Helping Hands

by Susan Ring

Consultant: Dwight Herold, Ed.D., Past President,
Iowa Council for the Social Studies

Yellow
Umbrella
Books
for early readers

Yellow Umbrella Books are published by Red Brick Learning
7825 Telegraph Road, Bloomington, Minnesota 55438
http://www.redbricklearning.com

Editorial Director: Mary Lindeen
Senior Editor: Hollie J. Endres
Senior Designer: Gene Bentdahl
Photo Researcher: Signature Design
Developer: Raindrop Publishing
Consultant: Dwight Herold, Ed.D., Past President, Iowa Council for the Social Studies
Conversion Assistants: Jenny Marks, Laura Manthe

Library of Congress Cataloging-in-Publication Data
Ring, Susan
 Helping Hands / by Susan Ring
    p. cm.
 ISBN 0-7368-5840-7 (hardcover)
 ISBN 0-7368-5270-0 (softcover)
 1. Community development—Juvenile literature. I. Title.
 HN49.C6R56 2005
 307.1'4—dc22
                                              2005015616

Photo Credits:
Cover: PhotoDisc Images; Title Page: Brand X Pictures; Page 2: Tom & Dee Ann
McCarthy/Corbis; Page 3: Brand X Pictures; Page 4: Jim West/ZUMA Press; Page 5: Cat
Gwynn/Corbis; Page 6: Jim West/ZUMA Press; Page 7: Jose Luis Pelaez, Inc./Corbis; Page 8:
Jim West/Photographer Showcase; Page 9: Pornchai Kittiwongsakul/Agence France Presse;
Page 10: Paula Bronstein/Getty Images, Inc.; Page 11: Larry Williams/Corbis; Page 12: Jose
Luis Pelaez, Inc./Corbis; Page 13: Rob Lewine/Corbis; Page 14: Lucas Oleniuk; Toronto
Star/ZUMA Press

1 2 3 4 5 6 11 10 09 08 07 06

Table of Contents

People Helping People

We can help other people in many ways.
We can help by doing simple things. We
can carry heavy bags. We can help
others cross the street.

We can also help each other by working together. Let's take a look at people helping others in different communities.

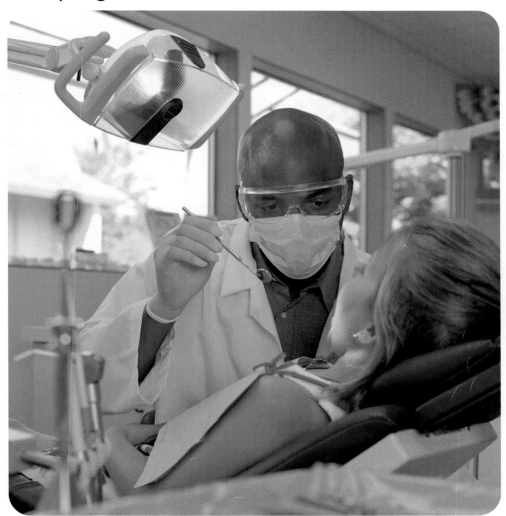

Let's Grow a Garden

People in this neighborhood are planting a **community garden**. The garden is in the middle of a busy city. Everyone lends a hand.

Everybody enjoys the garden. Many people visit it every day. It is a nice place to sit and read. The garden makes the neighborhood a better place to live in.

Let's Build a House

People in this community are building a house. Everyone lends a hand. Some people build the floor. Some build the roof.

One family is moving into the house. They will make it their home. People welcome them to the neighborhood.

Let's Paint a Wall

People in this community are painting a **mural**. Everyone lends a hand. Some people paint. Some wash the brushes.

Everybody enjoys the mural. People see it every day as they walk by. It is very colorful. The mural makes the neighborhood a better place to live in.

Let's Clean Up

People in this community are cleaning up the beach. They want to stop **pollution**. Everyone lends a hand.

Many people visit the beach every day. They swim or take long walks. A clean beach makes the neighborhood a better place to live in.

Let's Teach Others

This person is teaching this boy to become a better reader. She also takes time to **tutor** other kids with their homework.

These people are learning to speak English. The teacher enjoys giving her time to help them. People in a community can learn a lot from each other.

Let's Take a Ride

These people are taking a long bike ride. They are riding in a **bike-a-thon**. The more miles they ride, the more money they will raise to help other people.

It doesn't matter who comes in first. Everyone is a winner when people in a community help each other.

Glossary

bike-a-thon—a bike ride in which people ride their bikes to raise money

community—a neighborhood shared by many people

community garden—garden built and cared for by people who live in the same neighborhood

mural—large wall painting

pollution—things that make the water and air dirty

tutor—to teach

Index

Word Count: 327
Early-Intervention Level: J